i'll leave you with this

Makenna Misuraco

If you think it's about you,
it probably is.

Part I:

Bright Eyes

I think it was a Tuesday.

I think it was a Tuesday that I acknowledged your beauty for the first time.

The thought of my lips touching your skin

brought me to my knees.

I never understood how the thought of being with someone could be so enthralling

until I imagined how blissful it would be

to have you that very moment.

Day by day I'm learning you-

       and you amaze me in ways that I struggle to comprehend.

My thoughts never seem to come out right on paper,

but I will try until I can write words

that are half as remarkable

as you have made me feel.

Life crept up on me

through the back door-

Next thing I knew,

there was a person

who lit the fire

in my eyes;

with a presence

that made my bones

.

jumpstart.

Your smile reminds me

that I am only human.

A weak one

at that,

but only for you.

I met her just as summer was beginning-
I can still picture the sunlight
bringing out each individual freckle
across her face.

Sometimes I wonder how she can be so sad
when she is so beautiful.

There is so much hidden within her.
A whole other word that is strong enough
to build an empire,
or powerful enough
to completely tear mine down.

My temptations test me
to explore the mystery
of what is unknown-
     and I am trying to calculate the stillness
         that lies within the hurricane she holds,

but I worry that if I get too close,
     I'll get lost
     in the chaos of it all.

And here you are

consuming

all of the small,

empty,

     s p a c e s

of my mind.

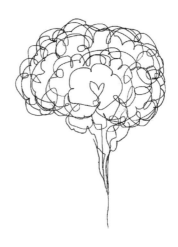

I knew I loved you-

when I sat across from you on your couch

that very first night we met.

We played drinking games

to break the tension,

 so we could find enough courage

 to exchange our first kiss.

I knew I loved you-

when we stayed in bed for 3 days

and binge watched

an entire crime documentary series.

We barely spoke,

but your presence brought me so much safety.

I knew I loved you-

when we spent New Years Eve together on my couch,

because we didn't want to go out.

So, instead we spent the night

consumed in each other's laughter-

playing one on one beer pong

        (and even though I lost every game)

It was my favorite way to ring into the New Year,

        Because I was with you.

I knew I loved you-

when we called things off,

because feelings were developing

and we agreed from the beginning,

that this was simply, "for fun".

I knew I loved you-

when I found myself in the arms of another

and I couldn't shake the thought

of missing you.

I knew I loved you-

when I heard you were seeing someone else

and the thought that you could share

those very same moments

made my stomach turn.

The truth is,

I have loved you all along.

I have loved you this entire time

And you have not even the slightest clue,

because I still

haven't told you.

Until now.

You laid in my lap and slow music played through the TV in the background.

    I ran my fingers through your hair.

        You looked up at me and smiled.

We didn't say anything,

but I knew we both felt it.

That we would've given anything

        to stay right there

                in that moment.

Magnets.

If she's positive,

I'm negative.

We're constantly being pulled together.

If you tried to get me to leave,

you would actually feel the resistance.

It's as if we're stuck together

through a force,

that neither of us can understand.

You can't see it.

But wow,

you can feel it.

(b.m.)

I hope you and I are each other's,
"happily ever after."

You should know,

I tend to be an impatient person.

I jump into things before I'm ready

and I say, "I love you."

before I mean it.

You've changed something in me-

      things are different here.

      But as long as it's you

      standing at the end of it all,

            I'm okay with waiting.

8 am-

She rolled over and kissed me gently,

almost as if she missed me while

we were sleeping.

She put her hand on my chest

and buried her face into my neck,

and I ~~hoped~~

> *prayed*

that this was what the beginning

of what forever

looked like.

Before we met,

I wonder if we spent the same nights

gazing up at the stars,

longing for a love

that would never break-

I wonder if you wished for me

the way I wished for you.

I want you to be the final chapter
of my love story;

one that I don't have to write
an ending to.

Your hands feel like safety-
as they wrap around my hips
and you kiss the back of my neck.

Your arms feel like shelter-
as we lay on the roof of my car
and you pull me in closer.

I hope you know how much I cherish those small moments.

That being with you
wherever we are,

always feels like home.

I love your scars.

They show you're not afraid to bleed–

To heal–

To try again.

I have such a hard time explaining my feelings to you.

(I even struggle to write them down.)

I sit here and try to come up with some type of metaphor or analogy.

(None of them do it justice.)

So as soon as the English language creates a word,

(That is even half as radiant as you make me feel.)

I will write them into books that I hope you will read.

(Scribble them onto pages until they're perfect.)

And hopefully then you will fully understand it all.

(How loving you has made me speechless.)

I wake up with hangovers,

next to strangers in the morning.

For some reason, I find more comfort in that,

than in the person who wants to stay.

The games are getting old and I'm tired of pretending that I don't care about you.

That I don't crave you.

That I don't want to see

what we could build together.

I know we could be great,

because we already are

but please know,

I am so terrified.

Inhale my love,

I'll exhale

your struggles.

You say hello

like there are no goodbyes

left in the world

and I become drawn to the thought

of never watching you leave.

You kiss me

and it takes the color out of the sky

and paints my life a masterpiece

that you are the focus of.

I look at you

and I am reminded of love

and what it feels like

to finally

be loved back

in return.

She believed in God,
  Hell,
  Angels,
  and miracles.

I believed in medicine,
  karma,
  sceptics,
  and good luck.

So it was weird
to hear myself say,
I would sit with her at church on Sunday morning-
when I hadn't been in 7 years.

It didn't have anything to do with religion, though.

It was because I believed in
  her
and she believed in
  me.

And together
we believed in
  loyalty,
  teamwork,
  sacrifice,

and love.

.

I know I'll wake up with you in the morning,

but I still hate to tell you goodnight.

Kiss every part of me,

so my skin

never gets the chance

to miss you.

I dream of holding you

for longer than

a few

      fleeting

moments.

She had a tendency to chase sunsets

    dreams,

        and people.

Some a little farther out of reach than others,

    but I hope at some point she is able

    to hold them all-

And learn that

the sun will always be back the next morning,

dreams will always be met as long as you keep fighting,

and not everyone you meet has to be in passing,

    because some people genuinely want to stay.

-You deserve them all.

She wears depression

like a makeover

and everyone around her

thinks she is simply

too beautiful,

to carry

so much sadness.

I'm not sure how you managed

to keep me going

and keep me from going.

I'll kiss you,

without a care in the world,

because one day we'll grow old

and laugh-

that we were once worried

about what people would say.

When I think

of

true beauty,

I hear the sound

of

your voice.

In this world full of chaos,

you seem to be the only thing

that makes

any

sense.

The truth is

darling,

I am trying so hard

not to think about you

that it is

all

I can do.

I have questioned my faith

my entire life-

     not knowing where to turn

     or who to pray to.

And no,

I can't compare her to religion,

but there was something about her eyes

that made me believe in something bigger again.

And *not* loving her,

well that would be

the biggest sin of all.

She wanted beautiful words
that described how much she meant to me,
but all I had left
were broken promises
from love I held before her.

So, I collected what was left
and tried to form a sentence
half as beautiful as her.

And what I came up with was,

You make me feel whole again.

Paint my life

with the

c o l o r s

of you.

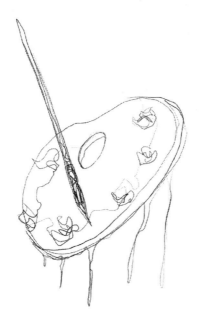

I have always thought that falling in love
was a mistake,

      but you have made it

      a chance worth taking.

You remind me

of my favorite song.

The track I could listen to

on repeat,

for hours

and the second it's over

I'm saying,

"Play it again."

I'm discovering myself as I discover her.

Your eyes are the sky;

     Azure

           meets

                    infinity.

     And when ours lock,
     I find myself helpless.

          Continuously

        lost

               in

        clouds

              of you.

I'm afraid of being vulnerable-

I'm afraid to give her
the pieces of myself
that I have protected for so long.

That if our eyes meet,
I'll fall for a part of her
I can't hold on to.

What if I give too much away
and I can't get any of it back?

I'm afraid of being vulnerable-
but I am trying.

I wish these hours would move slower.

I wish time wasn't a concept in my life.

(Thoughts I have while looking at you.)

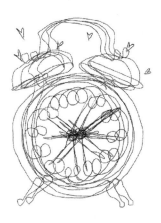

A temporary bliss,

some would call it-

but we

> *are not.*

Learning you

was rediscovering

all of my favorite words.

Loving you

is poetry.

In attempts to get to know her,

I asked her all of her favorite things.

> *Traveling.*
>
> *Coffee.*
>
> *Marvel.*
>
> *Crawfish.*

In the same breath,

I asked to list what she *loved* the most.

> *Her family.*
>
> *Writing.*
>
> *Being alone.*
>
> *Thor.*

The answer I was looking for was never spoken.

> *I wanted her to love herself.*

She grew up a Pastor's daughter,

using her beauty as competition

and as a tactic to be the best.

Men fell for her,

thinking they'd be able to hold her attention

for longer than the alcohol in her system stayed present.

No one cared to notice the bruises.

They didn't see her abusing pills behind the camera-

or slicing her thighs in the comfort of her bedroom.

I hope you know that I see you.

So, give me your madness.

I will take your damaged and broken-

and watch you flourish into

    someone beautiful

rather than

    something beautiful.

These hands were created

to hold yours

and I have no intention

on ever

letting go.

I have seen some of the most extraordinary things

this Earth has created.

Places so beautiful,

you forget how to breathe

when you look at them.

And none of them,

not one,

compares to the way I feel

when I look at you.

And I love you-

One thousand more ways
than I'll ever be able
to write down.

(But I'll keep trying until the words make sense.)

Timing has never worked out in my favor,

but I get this feeling every time I glance over at her

in my passenger seat,

singing,

with the windows down.

No, this feeling might not be everlasting,

One day she may decide to collect her things and go,

but I'll never forget the way

she made her way into my veins.

Like a drug

I was destined to be addicted to

on the first dose.

And if you go,

please cause a scene before you do.

Wreck the furniture-

Shatter the glasses.

I want to remember the chaos

and smile,

when I look back

to tell the story

of us.

I don't know how to tell you

I'll miss you

when you leave-

So I hope you felt it

in how

   l o n g

I kissed you

   goodbye.

I know we're constantly separated by distance,

so I hope it makes sense

when I say

that sometimes,

I can feel you

right next to me.

Empty-

is what a life without love,

     your love

would be.

A life without you,

would be more silence than laughter,

more storms without sunshine,

more songs with no melody.

A life without love,

     your love-

is something I could never

     comprehend.

My hands cramp

at the thought

that one day this ink

could be bleeding

for you.

You understood the madness

of what lied within

the hands in front of you-

And you stayed

anyway.

-Courage

If I could put my love for you

into ~~inches~~

     miles-

We would travel the entire solar system.

We'd stand on the rocks of the Moon,

     find water on Mars,

          run across the plains of Jupiter,

               freeze on Neptune,

                    burn with the Sun.

Once we returned to Earth,

we would have to do it all again.

And then maybe,

     maybe,

my love for you would be justified.

I have finally found someone

who has given me

something worth fighting for

and

all of the right reasons to stay.

(you.)

I forget what my life was like before knowing you.

(Something along the lines of trying to finish this poem,
but having nothing else to say.)

i'll leave you with this

Part II

False Perception

Can you feel it in your chest-

When you read the words that are about you?

Wake up my mind.

It's drifting to places

I can't find you in.

I use to take the long way to the bar,

because I couldn't stand to walk by

that city apartment we shared-

with that *stupid fucking green door*

and the side gate

that we'd lift each other over

when we forgot our keys.

I walked by it last week

for the first time in 10 months.

I could still hear your laugh echo

from our second story bedroom,

but it didn't make me sad

like I thought it would.

It reminded me

that all beautiful things

have a time and place

and that

was *ours*.

I have so many reasons

why I should go,

but I'll stay for the one

that

starts and ends

with you.

I don't understand how the person I loved

more than *anything*

in this entire world

slipped right through my fingertips,

and never even cared enough

to say

goodbye.

I wish I could call you.

Hear your honey sweet smile

and infectious laugh,

through the phone.

     For only a moment.

I wish we could catch up.

See how our families are.

We were in love once,

     weren't we?

How do I void the memory

of my first hug with your mother?

Laughing with your friends?

Experiencing the feeling,

     "This might be it."

And in the same breath,

it was all gone.

     You were gone.

I just *fucking wish*

I could tell you,

     I'm thinking of you.

"I want you to know I am walking around with a whole piece of myself missing."

-Me too.

I keep you alive

through the words I write-

Through my first book,

through this chapter,

and all of the ones to follow.

As long as I put my pen

to paper,

you'll never be gone.

As long as I continue to bleed my secrets to these pages,

our story will never end.

I can't still miss you.

I can't ~~still~~ miss you.

I ~~can't~~ still miss you.

I ~~can't still~~ fucking miss you.

I hear thunder approach
from miles away.
Rain pelts off my bedroom window,
as the foundation of my home
shakes from the storm.

The lights flicker.
Total blackout.
I am stuck in darkness.
Waiting for the power
to come back,
so we can exist again as normal.

I'm reminded
of when we were in our own storm-
You felt like miles away,
but somehow you shook me to my core.
I sat in darkness,
waiting for your lights to surge again,

but they never did.

My therapist knows everything about you

and I'm sure your ego will take that as a compliment.

-Maybe it is.

I stay up past midnight,

with more liquor

pumping through my veins,

than I am proud to admit.

I list out the reasons,

any at all,

to stay distant from you.

And none of them

are good enough to convince me,

that I wouldn't love it if you called.

-I miss your voice.

Hold me like a promise you can actually keep.

You ask me
if I'll write you into books.

If I'll paint butterflies with words
that describe how beautiful we were,
while doubling as something fragile
and short lived.

The answer is yes.
I am writing our delicacy into **this** book.

But more importantly,
        are you reading it?

                -Other people will assume this is about them.

You are dangerous to me-

Kissing me,

with no regard for how you'll feel tomorrow.

God,

I could not get over how beautiful you were.

I craved to know you,

       to hear what your voice sounded like.

I took my time.

Tried to explore each shadowed corner

of your mind-

To discover what makes you, you.

You pushed back on me,

       "You would be scared if you knew what existed in my mind."

But I wasn't in the slightest afraid of what there was to know.

The last few moments we spent together,

       you were once again, buried behind your walls-

          Distant.

You wouldn't budge.

You gave me nothing to work with,

       as if you didn't want me to understand you.

But in the end,

it all made sense:

       Not even you,

          understood yourself.

Everything beautiful in life

comes with a consequence

And

mine was

    you.

I can still hear you laughing from my passenger seat.

When I miss you,
I roll my windows down
and listen to your favorite songs.

I hope they still make you
as happy as they did
when you were beside me.

From the outside

my favorite city

is made up of colorful buildings,

beautiful people,

and loud noises.

With a closer look

It's filled with live music,

starving artists,

and a maze of streets.

A left will take me to a black out.

A right will take me to the river.

But if I can convince my feet

to move straight forward,

it might just bring me back to you.

And if I make it there,

there is no turning around.

My favorite city

Is the one where I can find you closest to.

No, it's not my favorite because of you,

but you being there

is one hell of a plus.

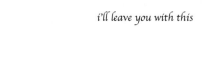

Hell is realizing we will never laugh together the way that we used to.

We were so short

and ever so sweet-

I can still taste the tequila on your lips-

and the fake,

"I love you"

rolling off your tongue.

Every kiss more intoxicating

than the last

and each word

      harder to believe.

      -March 14, 2020

I lay on her chest

and I can feel your heart break,

as I fall asleep

to the sound of her heartbeat.

-You always told me distance would make my love stronger

I drink myself into blackouts,

so your name doesn't slip off of my lips.

I'll Invite a stranger home-

Kiss them a few seconds too long-

Give them every reason to think I'll call back the next day.

But I remember waking up one morning,

wondering where you were-

Whose hands you found yourself in,

and if you regretted it

as much as I did.

- I miss us.

I feel like the universe pulled us apart

before we even got the chance

to explore

how much greatness we could create,

together.

There was a Big Bang

and the exploding stars in your eyes

turned to black holes.

I used to wonder

where the hell we went wrong.

And now,

I can't help but wish

we could have had

a few more moments.

Here's the thing

they never tell you about love;

You have no idea what angle it will hit you from,

but it will knock the wind from your lungs

And when they leave,

it stops your breathing

altogether.

Not once did I think you would have impacted me the way you did.

Each word you said, causing me to constantly lose sleep.

Wondering if your love was genuine,

Or if you felt obligated, because people were watching.

Running around my mind in circles-

Looking for clarity-

Even if what's true, hurts me.

And if that's what it takes for me to move on,

Name them. List them. Tell me.

So I can peacefully sleep again.

You exist in my mind as a distant memory-

And sometimes when I concentrate hard enough,

I can still feel your lips

brushed up against mine.

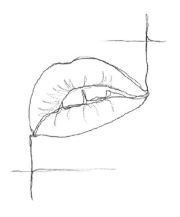

I have never considered myself
an insecure person.

I have always been sure
of who I am.

But I would be lying,
if I said,
I didn't feel uncertain of myself
around *you.*

Not "worthy"
of you.

And inferior
to you.

-And that's bullshit.

I can't help but go numb when I think about you-

filling empty cracks I once lived in

      with *strangers,*

that have nicer smiles

and stronger hands.

You send old photos of us to my phone-

        Kissing in the park.

        Asleep in my bed.

        Drunk smiling at my sister's 21st birthday.

I don't know what I am supposed to say.

        What do I do with this?

        What does this mean?

        How should I take it?

You left me

and all I can think

is that this is a manipulation tactic,

        to keep me close to you.

-Tell me the truth, for once.

When you are no longer my last thought

before I fall asleep,

I will know then,

that I'm over you.

I don't think

I will ever fully accept

that this story

doesn't end

with you and I.

You texted me

and told me we would be better as,

"Companions."

"Friends."

I still don't know what that means,

considering I saw you less than 72 hours ago

and I can still taste you

on the roof of my mouth.

So I'm not quite sure what kind of

"friendship"

you're looking for.

And when you kissed me,

I felt myself

drowning

in every breath

I took.

What I want

and what's best for me

are two different things.

Two separate entities,

with different names.

I know that lying with her at night

           is safe.

I know she wants to stay.

                    She plans to stay.

What does it say of the person I am,

to hope if you're thinking of me

as often as I'm thinking of you?

Because she wants me and *she has plans,*

       but I have always been in love

          with wanting things I can't have.

I find myself consumed in the thought

of you,

more than I am proud to admit.

I haven't heard from you in 2 weeks.

    I wonder if you think of me-

    if I ever cross your mind.

Sometimes I sit and try to convince myself

    that I miss you

    and that I'd like it if you called.

I keep trying to tell myself that what we were,

    for that *very* brief period of time,

    was love-

    But in the back of my mind

    and at the pit of my stomach,

I know it was only

    l u s t.

And you can tell people

we were a waste of time,

but I will always think

you were worth

every bit of my fight.

The next time I ask you,

    if you still love me,

      please,

        please

    fucking lie to me.

I wonder who I'd be
if I had never been introduced
to two arms that replaced my idea
of what makes a home.

A once strong foundation
now stands behind us,
and has become a *tedious* war-
composed of broken knuckles
and empty bottles of whiskey.

I placed a cigarette between my lips
to burn your taste away,
but I never had the courage to light it-

because no matter how hard I try to avoid it,
you were the fuel to my fire
and there's just no spark
without you here.

I touched you

with every intention

of holding on-

And you let go

with no intention

on

coming back.

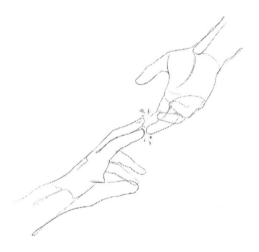

I didn't know withdrawal

until I watched you get up

and walk away from me.

No-

I wouldn't call her

"love."

I was just

"in love"

with the idea

of no longer

loving

y o u.

-Rebounds.

I write poems

about abusing alcohol-

like it's a luxurious

part of my life;

but each sip

cuts my throat

and I curse your name

as the chaser.

I scream into empty pages of notebooks,

because I can't seem to articulate

how fucking sad you make me.

I would let you break my heart

    1,000 times,

        if it meant I would still have you.

-The saddest truth.

I should have held you longer,

but I didn't want you to see me cry.

Or know how much I'd miss you

when you were gone.

So I cut our goodbye short

and got on the plane-

Not knowing that would be the last time

I'd ever see you.

Your eyes don't shine the way they used to when you look at me.

Weeks go by that I don't hear from you-

When I do,

you talk to me like

I'm still the one.

We'll catch up-

Family and friends.

Life and work.

Exchange a few laughs

and flirtatious comments.

But it hurts,

having to remind myself

that you only do this

because you're sad

and lonely-

And you know I will always answer.

What would my life look like if
I had gotten everything I've wanted?

Would I have you?

Loving you—

was taking a constant blow

to the chest

and forcing my knees

not to buckle.

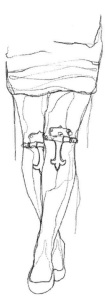

The last time I saw you replays in my mind like a broken record.

I can't stop replaying it.
I wish I could unfeel you-
    Crying into my shoulder.
    Telling me you love me.
    Holding me so tight
        that I almost lost oxygen-

        It was the kind of hug you give
        when you don't want to let someone go,
            but you have to.

And when you didn't say,
    "I'll see you soon."

        I knew it was our final goodbye.

Do I love you because I am lonely-

Or am I lonely because I love you?

We built ourselves an empire,

but fate couldn't stop us
from burning it
to the ground.

I watched the hours today go by like they were nothing.

One minute I looked up

and it was pitch black in the middle of the night.

And after I wondered,

Is this how easily you go through days without me?

(b.m.)

It didn't matter how hard I fought.

How much I tried.

How much love I gave.

You were never meant to stay.

I wish I would have known

that loving you,

would introduce me

to loneliness.

My life continued after you,

but it never felt the same.

Were demons telling you
     to pour salt
     all over my bloody wounds?

Turn my tears
     into acid,
so each one burned more
than the last
as they rolled down my face?

Pour alcohol
     down my fucking throat?

I can't think of you anymore.
     I won't.

That night is still blurry,
I can't seem to remember
if the bleeding,
the crying,
or the liquor,
made my body hit the floor first.

But I do know one thing-
I woke up the next morning
     and felt
     exactly the same.

(k.k)

You will never know how painful it was

to be on the receiving end

of

your

"love."

I have missed you
and on my worst days,
I still do.

I wrestle with the reality
of how things use to be
versus where we are now-
both seem to leave me

drunk

and a bit confused.

I have missed you,
but I'm not quite sure
who it even is that I'm lost in-
because my mind has created a version of you
that doesn't exist.

Only time will help me move on
and I'm confident that one day I will,
but do know,

I miss you.

I need to give this pain a place to call home.

You don't know,

how many nights we've spent together

that I almost slipped up

and said,

      "I love you."

I could have blamed it

on the alcohol,

like you and I

always do.

We both know

our connection is more

than we play it out to be,

but fate isn't doing us any favors in this lifetime.

So, instead,

I'll let you kiss me

with vodka remnant on your lips,

and you can keep pretending

that you don't actually care.

       -   Just *"friends"*

Tell me things I know I shouldn't believe.

Lie to me,

say you'll never leave.

(b.m.)

I hear your voice

And for a second

I swear that I'm okay.

I feel present-

My worries and anxieties

dissipate entirely.

I hear your voice

and for a second

you're still next to me.

I can feel you pressed up against my ear

as your hands pour down my skin.

I wish I had it in me to respond

because you without fail,

make me feel the most grounded.

But it's a cheap forgery

when I know you'll never stay.

-It's time I cleared my voicemail

You were this concrete person in my life.

People came,

and went,

and dissipated;

but the figure of *you*

stood strong in the ground-

Never altering from the weather,

or the abuse.

And I *thought* I knew

exactly

where I belonged.

Call us whatever you want,

I just need you here

tonight.

I wish you would've stopped yelling

for *one goddamn second-*

to touch me,

      hold me,

            kiss me;

because even when everything was

so terribly wrong,

your hands always felt so right.

If our love was nothing but a game,

then we both played to lose.

(And we did.)

I miss you,

but I am so relieved

you're not here.

You came as quickly as you left-
Like waves brushing up
against the shoreline,
with no intention of staying.

I disregarded
the heartache I would feel-
How you could kiss me hard
and be gone so quickly.

I should've remembered,
the ocean is miles long in depth
and there is so much to explore
beyond the surface level.

It may have taken me some time,

but I've finally learned

how to live with the thought of you

and not have it

tear me to

| **p** | **i** | **e** | **c** | **e** | **s** |

I've been better since you left-

but there are still nights

I wake up sweating.

Thinking of who could be lying next to,

holding,

and loving,

in the outline that my body created on your mattress.

I've been better since you left-

but there are still times

I walk the streets

with my hands at my sides

and grab onto the air accidentally;

anticipating

I'd be grabbing onto you.

I've been better since you left-

but there are still moments

where I sit on my kitchen floor and cry;

In the same spot where you'd touch my hips

and make me dance with you

in the refrigerator light.

I have been better since you left.

I'm not great,

but I'm better.

I've learned a lot from you,

but walking away

has been

      by far

the most useful.

I crave a love

that doesn't leave me

in the morning.

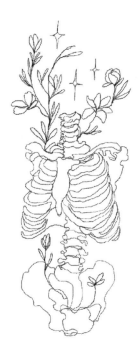

You chose to leave.

Please stop coming back around

when you feel empty.

I wasn't able to fulfil you then.

So now, it's my choice to decide.

And I no longer wish

to try,

to be what you need anymore.

My sleepless nights no longer

have your name

stained across them.

I tiptoed around your every move,

trying to stay silent when I had my own opinions,

throwing my hands in the air, to surrender to you.

I no longer wish to be a victim of the game

you *cheaply* label as "love."

So, I hope you take it

to whatever heart

you might have

when I tell you,

The best thing you could have

ever

done for me,

was walk away.

I wasted

months

of my life

wasted

off the thought

of missing

you.

You painted stars in my skies.

Made promises to me
that I was too naive to know,
        you could never keep.

I whitewash them out.

Start with a fresh canvas,
because you don't get to decide
        what shades I use.

I will create this journey alone
and construct beautiful masterpieces.

And you will have no say
in what color
        my skies turn out to be.

<u>I am sorry</u>

that the words I write for you

are no longer beautiful,

because I swear there were times

that you made me feel like

I created the stars in the sky.

I guess in time,

we both lost our way

and no matter how many times

I drew out the North star,

we could never find

our way back home.

I could feel your breath

pass through me-

Like trains.

    Waves.

    Thunderstorms.

Loud.   Abrupt.

    T e m p o r a r y.

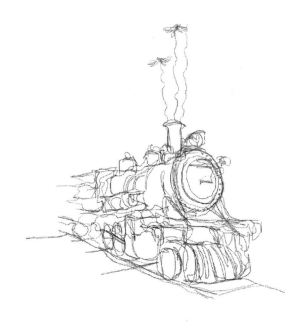

I couldn't heal from you,
until I let it hurt.

I couldn't heal from you,
until I let myself
be alone.
Until my bedsheets knew
you were never coming back.
Until my lips knew
they would never feel
yours again.
Until my hands knew
they would never hold you again.

I couldn't heal from you,
until I let it hurt-
And I thought not having you
would have killed me,

but it didn't.

I wrote a whole damn book about you

and you never even cared about me

enough to read it.

You're an old flame-

It is time

I let you

burn out.

I've tried to write you goodbye,

but every step forward

feels like ten away from you-

and now I'm scribbling your name

       all over

the goddamn page.

(relapse.)

"I love you"

was a promise

we were never meant

to keep.

You're in the same spot where you stood,

when you told me you could find better than me.

I watch myself progress

and I see my life succeeding-

And there you are,

stagnant.

When it's late at night,

I listen to the rain

and wonder if it's you crying

as a reflection of the sky;

While I start to paint my bedroom walls

a different color,

so I am forced to stay on my feet.

Reminding myself

that change is good;

and

things,

feelings,

and people,

will pass just like this weather.

I poured myself into you.

Tried to bend,

warp,

alter myself;

to fit inside of the box,

you labeled as,

      "Perfection."

I need to accept,

that I was not the best for you,

but I do hope

you will find that person

one day.

And I hope even more,

I will have grown enough

by then,

to be happy for you.

I dream of you

and wake up angry at my mind;

For continuing to decorate you

as a perfect illusion.

One day i'll be old

and I'll talk about you-

I'll tell my grandkids

about a great love

that knocked on my door,

but how life

had different plans for us.

one day I'll be old

and I'll talk about you-

I hope you'll talk about me, too.

I may have lost you,
but I found myself in the process
and I wouldn't give that up
for *anything*.

For the first time in my life

I feel like I am in control of my own feelings-

That I am able to love you,

and **not** want you back.

These will be the last words I write for you.

Know that I loved you-

Know that I forgive you-

but it is time for me to walk away.

And leave you,

and the memory of us,

on pages that will exist forever;

Even though we couldn't.

(P.S. They painted that green door black.)

i'll leave you with this

Part III

Tunnel Vision

Someone asked me today,

"Would the younger version of yourself be happy with who you've become?"

I thought for a second

and said,

"Probably not,

but I think she would understand."

(b.m.)

How can you be

so comfortable

living with

so

much

hatred

in your heart?

The scariest thing in the world,

is *not knowing.*

Not knowing how deep the ocean actually is.

or how infinite the solar system is.

Not knowing if tragedy is lingering, closely around the corner.

Not knowing who might be gone tomorrow.

Not knowing if the world will ever find some peace.

Not knowing if we'll ever truly be "safe."

Not knowing what is a figment of

your imagination,

versus what is actually reality.

Not knowing if the person you love,

loves you back.

      Regardless if they say they do.

Not knowing if you're good enough.

Or atleast good enough, to be something in this life.

The scariest thing in the world,

are all the things we will never know.

The things we will rarely get honest answers to.

I'm not asking you to wait for me,

but know I'm trying to get to you

and I'm almost home.

The universe tells me
that the odds will never be
in my favor,

but I am determined
to beat every statistic.

I am determined
to create something
so damn beautiful

that the planets stop rotating

just

to

stare.

The sun will rise

tomorrow

and so will

we.

Be the voice for those who are afraid.

Defend the people who don't get an equal say.

Stand tall.

Be loud.

      Scream.

The time for change

          is *now.*

If you run into the person I use to be,

please tell her-

I miss her.

I put us in a position where you had to walk away from me
and you have no idea how much I hate myself for it.

You know those video games

where every choice you make

affects the ending?

So you save your progress

at every checkpoint,

just incase the choice you make

kills you?

That's how I feel.

(b.m.)

The future of this world

is the product

of what

we allow ourselves to become.

I am not special.

    I know this.

I am one person,

with millions of flaws.

I bleed.

    I feel.

        I fail.

Please do not hold me up high.

I will disappoint you.

    I am someone ordinary,

        trying to help

        other ordinary people,

        feel like they belong.

When you get to heaven,

tell them I am someone worth saving.

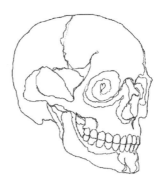

Impact my life.

Make me question who I am.

Make me want to change.

My soul will then move for you.

The true essence of beauty
is being able to look
your body in the mirror

  and be proud

    of the skin

      you were born in.

A part of growing up is learning that some people will never be happy for you, because they're so unhappy with their own lives.

-Growing pains.

I enjoy falling in love

with girls who don't care-

There is something comforting

about

   n e v e r

having to get

comfortable.

I have had long days.

      I think it's important for you to know, I have had some long fucking days.

      Some even feel longer than 24 hours- those are the worst.

      Like the universe is testing me to see how much more I can bear.

      I'm tired of every day feeling like a *goddamn war*

      that I am the only one fighting in.

      I'm alone on the battlefield, face to face with a mirror;

      I shatter it, to remind myself that **I will not break** just as easily.

I know it wasn't my fault, but I still feel myself getting tense at the thought of handsy strangers.

      I am not a product of your mistake, or your lack of self control.

I am a product of a woman empowered society-

      A strong one at that.

The days might drag and the nights may sting,

but I feel your hands on my skin and your breath on my neck

less each day.

And with this I have learned

      I am,

          shatterproof.

I will lay with my mistakes,

      greet them in the morning,

      as the sun kisses my face.

And promise myself

that today

      I'll try a *little harder,*

to be better

than I was

      yesterday.

I'm not fast.

But sometimes,

I wish

I could

   r

      u

         n

so far away from myself,

that not even my shadow

would have a chance

to

catch

      me.

Alcohol

made my life a nightmare-

but honestly,

it's the only thing

that helped me

sleep peacefully

at night.

I hope the love I give

to others

travels deeper than the love I give

myself.

I am aware

that actions always speak louder than words,

so I'm sorry my actions,

spoke the worst of me.

And mostly,

I'm sorry that I didn't know what I had,

until I didn't have *you* anymore.

I will learn to celebrate my own darkness.

Perhaps the moon
stays up all night
after hearing secrets
from the sun,
wondering if she will **eve**
find another lover,
who shines just as **bright**
as he.

i'll leave you with this

Vertically

      I cut to remind myself

      that I can still bleed.

      That I can feel anything at all.

Empty

      I searched for reasons to stay.

      I tried to remember how I got here,

      but came up with nothing.

      Only numbness.

Relief

      That someone cared enough.

      to pick me up off the ground.

      Clean me up.

      Mend my broken pieces and remind me:

I don't *need* to feel pain

to be *alive*.

That it's *okay*

 to feel *empty*.

That I am *grateful*

to have people *lift* me back up,

when I had *convinced* myself for so long,

      that I was nothing.

Behind every door

is a journey

waiting for you

to take

the next

step.

Imagine a world

where we could choose

who we love.

Am I happy?

Or am I going through the motions

with a fake smile on my face,

hoping no one looks close enough to notice?

You didn't have to yell

to kill her self esteem

and you didn't need to hit her,

push her,

or put your hands on her

to break her.

You did just as much damage

by telling her

you loved her

and not meaning it at all.

I'm sorry for the hearts
I haven't held gently.

For the ones I was reckless
and careless with.
For the hearts I tossed around.

I've been doing some reflecting,
     self-growth,
and during it I realized;

many of you helped me become
a better person.

And I'm sorry
you can't say the same.

I click my heels,

but I'm still stuck in this place

where people are getting

    hunted,

    killed,

    and buried;

While the privileged *swear*

    that our genders,

        races,

        and love,

            are all equal.

Wipe off your tears.

> *Wipe off your fucking tears.*

Get out of bed.

I don't even care,

if you're just going through the motions.

> *Fucking move.*

Dance alone in your apartment.

Sing.

No one is listening anyway.

We get one life.

One chance to make an impact.

One attempt to change people.

This is *mine*.

> This is *yours*.

My comfort zone became my worst enemy.

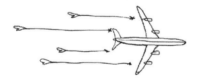

Sometimes, I struggle to express myself

in ways that are easy for other people to understand.

I think if people were able

to see inside of my mind,

they would be intimidated by the darkness-

and be afraid of how

one day i am flying,

happy.

And the next I am sinking,

dying.

You would probably think I'm crazy,

if you were able to crack me open

and know my every thought,

because trust me,

sometimes,

I think I am too.

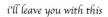

Let me be the voice behind the words you struggle to speak.

If ignorance is *truly* bliss;

Wipe my memory.

Take the smile from my face.

Let me live in a world

that is full of color.

Where there is

      no heartbreak,

            or pain.

We count success

based off of those around us.

The millionaires,

billionaires,

big houses and fancy cars.

      Luxury items.

My success

will forever be based

off of how I treat

the people around me.

      And how happy I am

            with myself.

And even if you don't choose me,

I will.

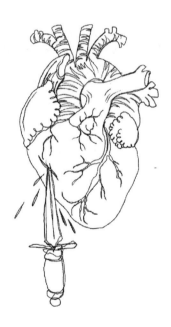

I will love the stars

loudly

and I will dance

bravely

under the night sky.

My soul illuminating through darkness,

casting a silhouette from the moon.

Though I am alone,

I have spent too many nights here

to ever be afraid.

I am myself,

I am safe,

And I will rest

at sunrise.

I gave so much love away,

but constantly felt empty-

Eventually I realized,

I hadn't saved any

for myself.

"I stared at the ceiling fan, wondering if it could hold my weight."

She said to me

with tears in her eyes,

as we drove down back roads in the city.

It was astonishing to me-

That she didn't understand the complexity of her beauty,

or the way she was capable of lighting up the room.

It was astonishing to me-

That we,

      as humans,

will let *another person*

determine the value of our excellence.

(Summer, 2019)

I often find myself a footnote

in other people's love stories.

(Will I ever write my own?)

I do my best to function properly-

> get out of bed,
>
> brush my teeth,
>
> eat breakfast.

Spend time with my friends,

> go to bars-
>
> go to the *fucking places* that I never,
>
>> *ever*
>>
>>> *want to be at.*

It's at that point
when breathing
becomes difficult.

And suddenly I'm surrounded by

> Unfamiliar faces.
>
> Insecurity.
>
> Overly crowded rooms.

My oxygen levels run low.
 I grip my fingers to my throat.
Feel my pulse to remind myself that I can still breathe.

What is this feeling?

Why do I struggle so hard?

Why can I never stop believing

that **this**

is where my story ends?

-Fuck anxiety.

I watched my mother

wrap her arms

around my fathers waist,

as he made coffee that morning.

I thought to myself,

how beautiful it was;

After 30 years of marriage

and sleeping next to each other every night,

she still hated

being away from him.

If I go before my time,

collect the words I have scribbled

into journals,

      diaries,

           notebooks.

Show the world

all of the unedited,

      honest words

           I have ever written.

Some say poetry
is for the lost souls,
but I have never felt
more visible—
more understood.

The better human in me

wants a start to a new life-

One where I am the captain of the ship

and the holder of my own destiny.

The bitter human in me

wants to be more than just a statistic-

A failed one, nonetheless.

The bigger human in me

wants a chance to be reborn-

To fight through the flames

and come out untouched.

The *honest* human in me,

knows we still have work to do,

but I'm on my way.

I'm sorry for the times I don't answer the phone-

Every so often, I get lost in my head.

    Most days, I feel gray.

And I'm left wondering

    if there really is a medication

to help me feel,

    like myself again.

    Or feel anything at all.

I can't put the blame on

anyone other than myself,

but I can't help but wonder;

    Would I would be okay,

        had I never met you?

I remember pulling away from my parents driveway and realizing it was the last time I could call it my driveway.

I remember moving into a home that needed my own memories to fill it.

I remember my first low point, and how much this place didn't feel like home.

I remember the first panic attack, where my roommates filled the void of the family I so desperately craved

I remember making a new home. A different kind of family.

I remember pulling into my own driveway.

I wish I knew how to be more present

in moments

that one day I'll look back on

and wish I could relive.

I screamed,

     "I love you."

down the valley,

just to hear my own **voice**

remind me

of my worth.

I have to admit this to you,

I am so tired

of trying to be good enough.

A good enough child.

A good enough sibling.

A good enough friend

     Partner.

          Writer.

My soul is tired.

     Please let me be me.

Children believe in magic,

the way adults believe in soulmates.

-A hopeful illusion.

I watched my best friend experience the most traumatic heartbreak of her life.

I held her hand as she broke down in the car-
slamming her fists into the steering wheel,
asking me,

  "What did I do to deserve this?"

I wished I had answers,
   but no encouraging words,
    would have made his actions okay.

I lifted her up under my arm
and carried her into our home.
  Barefoot.

I sat on the floor of her bathroom,
as she laid lifelessly on her shower floor;
Washed her back.
Wiped her mascara running tears.
Put her into an old oversized t-shirt.
Held her as her breathing stabilized again.

Neither of us ate or slept for 4 days.
  4 days.

And when she started to feel better,

I did too.

When she started sleeping and eating again,

      I knew it would be okay.

I knew she would be better, because of this.

My loyalty to you is unmatched,

because I know you'd do the same for me.

      Because you *do,*

      do the same for me.

      WE are a unit.

      My soul is *forever*

            intertwined with yours.

I tend to run from love when it's presented to me.

I think this is the outcome

of not wanting people to be close to me.

To learn me.

To know me.

-This is your disclaimer.

When you read this,

I hope you know

we will be okay.

I do not need to live a long life-

the length

and number of years

will not satisfy me.

I was put on this Earth

to leave an impression in the soil,

so when my footsteps are retraced,

you will know

I've been

h e r e.

I do this thing where I drink too much
and I start talking about all of my thoughts and feelings.

I know it can be annoying to sit and listen to me talk about a boy from the fourth grade,
who always chewed the top of his pencil-

And it's probably strange to see me cry over my dog who's still alive;
it's not because I'm sad, but because he saved my life-

And I'm sorry that I keep talking about my first love, but a part of me feels like if I don't,
I'll get hurt again just as badly.

I do this thing where I drink too much
and I start talking about all of my thoughts and feelings,

because most days I feel like I don't have a voice.

And all I've ever wanted
was for someone to really listen.

(Thank **you** for listening.)

i'll leave you with this

To my family,

friends,

supporters,

You make what I do possible.

I am not a poet without you.

Without your trust

in my words.

Without your belief in what I do.

To Jack Wild Publishing

and Dylan Carr,

thank you for

making my second book possible.

Here is to hopefully,

many,

more.

All my love & gratitude,

Makenna

Made in the USA
Middletown, DE
27 June 2021

First printing, 2020.
Jack Wild Publishing LLC
www.jackwildpublishing.com